T0021932

Who Is
Ken Jennings?

by Kirsten Anderson

illustrated by Jake Murray

Penguin Workshop

To my dad, Stanley Anderson, who was curious
and liked to learn about everything—KA

For Matt, Amanda, and the greatest
trivia team in the city!—JM

PENGUIN WORKSHOP
An Imprint of Penguin Random House LLC, New York

Visit us online at www.penguinrandomhouse.com.

Library of Congress Cataloging-in-Publication Data is available upon request.

ISBN 9780593226438 (paperback)   10 9 8 7 6 5 4 3 2 1
ISBN 9780593226445 (library binding)   10 9 8 7 6 5 4 3 2 1

Contents

Who Is Ken Jennings?

Ken Jennings wrote three words on his digital screen: *"Who is Jones?"*

Were those the right words? If that was the correct answer, he'd be a *Jeopardy!* winner, something he'd dreamed about all his life. If it wasn't, well . . . at least he had gotten to be on the game show he'd loved since he was ten years old.

It was February 24, 2004. Ken had led for most of the game, but Julia Lazarus, one of the other contestants, was close behind. If he answered wrong and she answered right, he would lose.

Jeopardy! is a quiz show that asks questions about trivia. The twist is that the "questions" are statements, and the "answers" must be phrased in the form of a question. This *Jeopardy!* question was "She's the first female track & field athlete to win medals in five different events at a single Olympics."

Ken hadn't watched any of the last Summer Olympics, in Sydney, Australia, in 2000. But he remembered hearing that Marion Jones, the American track star, had won a lot of events at Sydney. He was almost sure that she must be the correct answer. Just to be careful, he only wrote down her last name. Ken had played in a lot of trivia tournaments in college and knew that the safe thing to do was to write only a person's last name. He wouldn't want to lose because he made a mistake on a first name when he had the correct last name.

It was time to show his answer. The blue screen on his podium lit up with the words he had scrawled, "Who is Jones?" Alex Trebek, the host of *Jeopardy!* at the time, looked over at the table of judges who watch each game and make decisions if there's a question about a contestant's answer. Ken suddenly realized what was going on—Jones is a very, very common last name. His answer looked like it might be just a guess. The judges could decide he hadn't been clear enough. Then, all would be lost because he'd played it too safe.

After a pause that seemed to last forever, Trebek announced, "We'll accept that. You've got $17,000 more for a $37,201 total, and you become the *Jeopardy!* champion!" Ken had won his first game.

At the end of the next game, Ken won again. And again. And again. Americans tuned in every night, waiting to see if anyone or anything could trip up this master of trivia. Ken won *seventy-four* straight games in a row! After game seventy-five, he was sure of one thing: the answer to "He holds the longest winning streak in *Jeopardy!* history" was "Who is Ken Jennings?"

CHAPTER 1
What Is *Jeopardy!*?

Kenneth Wayne Jennings III was born on May 23, 1974, in Edmonds, Washington. His parents are Catherine and Kenneth Jr. For as long as he can remember, Ken liked to learn things and weird facts. His mother recalled bringing him to the University of Washington to be tested for a gifted and talented program. She overheard the testers ask him where the Wright brothers' first flight took place. Ken correctly answered, "Kitty Hawk, North Carolina." He was just four years old!

Ken was fascinated by books of trivia like the *Guinness Book of World Records* and *Ripley's Believe It or Not!* He memorized long lists of facts and recited them to anyone who would listen.

When it was time for him to start school, he was upset because that meant he would miss the daytime game shows that were another great source of oddball information.

When Ken was seven years old, his father, a lawyer, got a job in Seoul, South Korea. In Seoul, Ken attended a school for American children. The only American television shows available were on the Armed Forces Korea Network (AFKN). In 1984, when Ken was ten, AFKN began to run a quiz show called *Jeopardy!* on weekday afternoons. Soon it was the talk of Ken's school. Kids got together each day to go over the questions they'd seen on the show the day before. Ken dreamed that maybe someday he could be on *Jeopardy!*

But in middle school and high school, something became clear to Ken: Reeling off lists of facts and trivia made him seem like a know-it-all. He stopped buying trivia books and threw out the notebooks he'd filled with questions and answers he'd seen on old game shows. By the time he was a freshman in college at the University of Washington, he didn't even watch *Jeopardy!* regularly anymore.

As a member of the Mormon church, Ken was sent on a two-year mission to do volunteer work in Madrid, Spain. Ken then returned to the United States to finish college at Brigham Young University (BYU) in Provo, Utah. At BYU, he discovered a place where his love for trivia and being a know-it-all was actually useful: the college quiz bowl team. The quiz bowl team traveled to tournaments once or twice a month. In between, they prepped themselves by studying topics like lists of French kings or names of opera characters.

A BYU student won the *Jeopardy!* college tournament in 1994, and Ken got to meet him. The idea of actually being on *Jeopardy!* had always seemed so out of reach to him back when he was a fifth-grader in South Korea. But now here was someone who had really done it. Could he maybe, possibly, someday do it, too?

Jeopardy! Rules

Jeopardy! has three rounds: Jeopardy!, Double Jeopardy!, and Final Jeopardy! There are six subject categories in each of the first two rounds. Each category has five "clues," or questions. In the Jeopardy! round, clues are worth $200 to $1,000. In Double Jeopardy!, clues are worth $400 to $2,000. One of the twists of the game is that the clues are given in the form of statements, and contestants must give a reply in the form of a question—or it doesn't count.

Daily Doubles are hidden on the game board. They give contestants the chance to earn even more money.

After a clue is revealed, the first contestant to press their buzzer gets to answer the question. If their answer is correct, they win the value of that question, and they get to choose the next clue. If they get it wrong, they lose that amount.

In Final Jeopardy!, there is only a single clue. The contestants are shown the subject category and then place their bets based on that topic. They are given a clue and thirty seconds to write down their answer. If they are correct, they get to add that amount to their total score. If they're wrong, they lose that amount. The contestant with the highest score at the end of Final Jeopardy! is the winner and gets to keep the amount of money they've won. They then return to play another game.

The word *jeopardy* means "exposure to danger or trouble"—and the fast pace of the show and the many clues to solve certainly can make contestants feel as if they're in jeopardy!

CHAPTER 2
What Is a *Jeopardy!* Audition?

Ken graduated from BYU in 2000 with degrees in computer science and English. He married his girlfriend, Mindy Boam, whom he had met at BYU, and got a job working as a computer programmer in Salt Lake City. He and Mindy bought a house. Their son, Dylan, was born in 2002.

It seemed like everything was going fine. But secretly Ken disliked his job. He found the work incredibly boring. And he didn't think he was even a very good software programmer.

In the early 2000s, televised game shows had become very popular. *Who Wants to Be a Millionaire?* was a huge TV hit, and other game shows began to appear. Ken saw people he knew

from college quiz bowl tournaments winning on these shows, and he wondered if he could do it, too. He read that *Jeopardy!* held auditions every

few weeks in Los Angeles. He decided that the next time he was in the Los Angeles area, he would go to a *Jeopardy!* audition.

In April 2003, Ken and Mindy were planning to go to Southern California for a few days. Ken checked in with *Jeopardy!* and saw that they would not be holding auditions while he was in California. The next set of auditions would take place the following week.

Ken was disappointed. He didn't know when he'd have a reason to visit California again. He thought he'd have to put his *Jeopardy!* dreams aside.

But he didn't want to. So he came up with a new plan. Ken talked to his wife about the dates of the audition, and they agreed that they would make their trip to California as planned, and then the next week, he would go back to California for the audition. Earl Cahill, a friend from the BYU quiz bowl team, would join him.

The *Jeopardy!* audition was held at a hotel in Culver City. It began with a timed fifty-question test. Ken didn't know all the answers, but he thought he did pretty well.

The show's staff graded the tests, then read the names of the people who'd passed. Ken was nervous, but his name was on the list. Earl passed, too.

Next, they played a pretend game of *Jeopardy!* Ken knew that in this next part of the audition, the show's staff wanted to find out if the people who passed the test could follow directions and show their personality on television. They wanted contestants who were smart *and* entertaining. Ken made it through the interview section, telling a story about his baby son, but the other contestants seemed very lively and interesting. It was going to be hard to get on the show.

The *Jeopardy!* staff told Ken and the other contestants who passed that they were now in the show's contest pool. For the next year, they could get a phone call at any time telling them that they had been picked to be on the show. And if they didn't get that call? Well, they could audition again in a year.

For months, Ken waited for the call. Anytime he saw an unfamiliar number on his phone, he wondered if it might be *Jeopardy!* But no call came. As the days passed, he began to give up hope.

Then, one day in late January 2004, Ken's phone at work rang. The caller introduced himself as "Bob from *Jeopardy!*" They wanted Ken to be on the show.

CHAPTER 3
"Who Is Jones?"

Ken had less than a month to get ready for his appearance on *Jeopardy!* He recorded episodes of the show and watched them while standing behind a sofa. He thought that would get him used to the podium that contestants stand behind on the show.

One of his son's toys became a practice "buzzer." Ken knew that using the buzzer was one of the hardest parts of being on the show. Contestants have to wait until the host finishes reading the clue. Then there is a pause of a few beats before they can buzz in to try to respond with the correct question. If someone tries to buzz in too early, their buzzer will briefly stop working. Getting the timing right was important.

Alex Trebek (1940–2020)

George Alexander Trebek was born in Sudbury, Ontario, Canada. He got an early start in the world of broadcasting by working at the Canadian Broadcasting Company while he was still a student at the University of Ottawa. After graduating with a degree in philosophy, he had his first big break in 1963 as the host of a pop-music show called *Music Hop*. In 1966, he began to host *Reach for the Top*, a quiz show for high-school students.

Alex moved to the United States in 1973, and hosted a number of game shows throughout the 1970s. In 1984, he began to host a new version of *Jeopardy!*, a game show that had originally aired on American television in the 1960s.

Alex became known for his calm manner, sense of humor, and trademark mustache. Sometimes he gave the show's writers ideas for questions or categories. And if he thought a question was too hard, he let the writers know.

Alex hosted the show for thirty-seven years, taping episodes almost up until his death from cancer on November 8, 2020.

Many audience members assumed that Alex knew the answers to all the clues he read to the contestants. He said that of course he did—the answers were "written on a sheet of paper in front of [him]."

But Ken still had to know the answers to the questions. He made flash cards with facts in all kinds of categories: World leaders. Capital cities. Vice presidents. College mascots. Ken studied the flash cards constantly and had Mindy quiz him on them after he got home from work at his computer programming job.

Finally, the day came. *Jeopardy!* tapes ten games over two days in its Culver City studio—five shows each day. Ken was scheduled to be one of the contestants on either February 24 or 25. He drove from Utah back to Southern California.

Ken wasn't selected to play until the third game on the twenty-fourth.

The game seemed to happen much faster in person than when Ken watched the show on TV at home. There was so much going on: the lights, the cameras, the audience, reading the clues, timing the buzzer. *Jeopardy!* is a fast-paced game.

Each game packs up to sixty-one questions into less than half an hour.

Ken built up a big lead at first, but then Julia Lazarus, one of the other contestants, caught up. For the Final Jeopardy! round, Ken was ahead of her by only $2,000. She could easily beat him if he got the answer wrong in the Olympics category.

He didn't feel bad, though. While he had hoped to win at least one game of *Jeopardy!*, Ken thought he would be happy just as long as he made it to the Final Jeopardy! round and got to finish the game. And now he actually had a chance to win.

Then came the clue about Marion Jones, the Olympic five-medal winner. And Alex Trebek announced that they would accept Ken's simple answer—in the form of a question, of course—"Who is Jones?" Ken had won the game!

When he was young, Ken had never known what to say when people asked him what he wanted to be when he grew up. Now he knew

the answer to that question. He wanted to be a *Jeopardy!* winner. And now he was.

CHAPTER 4
What Is a Winning Streak?

Ken won his next two games. And then he won all five games the next day. His winnings for the two days came to $266,158.

He had to fly back to California the following week to tape at least one more show. Ken found it hard to believe that he could win another game.

But he won all ten games the next week! That meant he had to once again return to Los Angeles the following week.

That created a problem. What would he do about work? The games Ken was taping wouldn't actually appear on TV for months. *Jeopardy!* contestants aren't allowed to tell anyone whether they won or lost. Ken didn't even tell his parents.

But he had to tell his boss why he kept taking even more time off. She agreed to keep it a secret.

Ken went back to Los Angeles the next week and won *another* ten games. He kept winning throughout the spring. Still, no one knew his secret. Most of the time he was just Ken Jennings, ordinary computer programmer. But for a couple of days each week or so, he had another identity: Ken Jennings, supersmart trivia master, who broke *Jeopardy!* records with each game he won.

Some games were close. But he won many easily. Ken didn't think he was necessarily that much smarter than the other contestants. He guessed that he just had an advantage from having played the game before. He remembered his first game and how quickly it had moved. Many players who probably knew just as much as he did would spend the whole game struggling to get the buzzer timing down. Because it was now familiar to him, he felt more confident.

The episode featuring Ken's first game aired on television on June 2, 2004. He gathered all his friends and family to watch the episode in the

lobby of his office building. It was the first time any of them found out that he had won even one game. By that time, he had actually won forty-eight games! It was by far the longest winning streak in the show's history.

Now that the taped shows of Ken's wins were finally being shown on TV, people began to recognize him. They greeted him on the street or in grocery stores. Some people knew his name. Other just called him *Jeopardy!* Guy. The ratings for *Jeopardy!* went up, as more and more people began watching the show. They wanted to see how long the software programmer from Utah who seemed to know everything could keep the streak going.

Ken got requests for interviews and TV appearances. He was even on an episode of *Sesame Street.*

Jeopardy! winners don't receive any of their prize money until months after they have appeared on the show. So in between all the show tapings and interviews, Ken was still working at the office. It was a lot to manage.

In September 2004, Ken arrived in Los Angeles to tape more games. He won the first game that day. It was his seventy-fourth straight win. It wasn't easy, though. The seventy-fifth game was even harder. He made a few incorrect guesses on Daily Doubles and lost a lot of money on them. When they entered the Final Jeopardy! round, he knew that he was in danger of losing to contestant Nancy Zerg.

The category was Business & Industry. Ken was worried. That wasn't a strong subject for him.

The clue appeared on-screen:

"Most of this firm's 70,000 seasonal white-collar employees work only 4 months a year."

Thirty seconds ticked away as Ken tried to think of businesses that might only need employees for four months a year. Maybe it had something to do with the busy holiday gift season? He decided to go with FedEx, the package shipping company.

Nancy's response was revealed first. She had

written "What is H&R Block?" the company that prepared people's taxes. Alex announced that Nancy was correct. And she had bet enough that she was now ahead of Ken by $1.

Ken's incorrect question was revealed. The audience gasped. Ken's streak was over.

Ken had always known his winning run would come to an end someday. He was both sad and

relieved that it was over. On one hand, playing *Jeopardy!* was fun. But keeping up the streak had been stressful.

In between shows, host Alex Trebek didn't spend time with the contestants. So, although they had spent many days in the studio together taping the show, Ken had barely said a word to Alex off camera. He sometimes wondered if Alex was tired of him.

But after Ken's seventy-fifth game ended, Alex came over to him and said, "Congratulations, Ken. We're going to miss you around here."

Questions Ken Got Wrong!

Clues

1. In April 1939, this country absorbed Albania.

2. The closest country to Greenland is this one,
   a mere sixteen miles away.

3. Due to the efforts of Spokane resident Sonora
   Dodd, this holiday was first celebrated there,
   on June 19, 1910.

4. These names of two original Mercury astronauts,
   who orbited Earth in May 1962 and May 1963,
   are also occupations.

5. The name of this often brimless hat, popular in
   the 1920s, is French for "bell," after the shape
   of the hat.

Correct Answers

1. What is Italy?
2. What is Canada?
3. What is Father's Day?
4. Who are Cooper and Carpenter?
5. What is a cloche?

CHAPTER 5
Who Is the Greatest of All Time?

Ken's final episode aired on November 30, 2004. Overall, and because the show doesn't air on weekends, it took 182 days for all of Ken's episodes to be shown. *Jeopardy!* shows repeat episodes during the summer, and Ken's appearances were paused in the fall for some special tournaments. That meant that Ken's streak had been a suspenseful story for about six months! He was now America's most famous game show contestant. Many people considered him an expert on everything.

And he had won a total of $2,522,700. Ken tried not to let it change his life too much. The only thing he and Mindy really splurged on at first was a new big-screen TV.

Soon after appearing on the show, Ken took time off from his programming job to write a book, and he never went back. *Brainiac: Adventures in the Curious, Competitive, Compulsive World of Trivia Buffs* was published in 2006. Eventually, he and his family, which now included daughter Caitlin, moved to Seattle, and Ken became a full-time writer. He published books for both adults and children. He also wrote quizzes for a variety of magazines and websites.

Ken did have another job, though: game show contestant!

Ken came in second in 2005's *Jeopardy! Ultimate Tournament of Champions*, losing to Brad Rutter, *Jeopardy!*'s all-time highest earner. He also appeared on the game shows *1 vs. 100* and *Are You Smarter Than a 5th Grader?* (He was.) Ken served as an expert for contestants who wanted to "Ask an Expert" on *Who Wants to Be a*

Millionaire? Contestants tried to stump him with trivia on the "Stump the Master" portion of *GSN Live* on the Game Show Network.

In 2011, Ken was invited to take part in a special *Jeopardy!* event. He and Brad Rutter would compete in a series of games against IBM's new supercomputer, Watson.

Ken, Brad, and host Alex Trebek traveled to IBM's headquarters in Armonk, New York. Because the supercomputer was actually the size of a room and made too much noise to be anywhere near the show's taping, a large room at IBM was turned into a *Jeopardy!* studio. IBM employees were the show's audience. Watson was represented by a simple screen with flashing lights.

The computer processed information and buzzed in its answers much quicker than Ken and Brad. The IBM employees cheered every correct answer from the machine. By the end of two games (which were shown over three days), Watson had won $77,147. Ken came in second with $24,000.

In 2014, Ken competed in the *Jeopardy! Battle of the Decades* tournament, but lost again to Brad Rutter. In 2019, Ken was the captain of a team in the *Jeopardy! All Star Games*. His team came in second to Rutter's.

Then, in January 2020, Ken, Brad Rutter, and James Holzhauer came together to compete in the *Jeopardy! Greatest of All Time (GOAT)* championship. Holzhauer had won thirty-two straight games in 2019. He became famous for his daring style of play, where he chose the highest-value clues first and bet large amounts on Daily Doubles and Final Jeopardy!

Ken had usually played it safe when it came to the betting parts of *Jeopardy!*, but he knew that he would have to play like Holzhauer in order to beat him. Ken won the first game, and Holzhauer won the second. Then Ken won the next two games. That gave him the title of "Greatest of All Time." He also won $1,000,000.

Ken Jennings, James Holzhauer, and Brad Rutter

After adding that to the money he'd already won on *Jeopardy!* and other game shows, Ken became the highest-earning contestant in American game show history.

The Final Jeopardy! clue of the last game was: "He has 272 speeches, the most of any non-title character in a Shakespeare tragedy." Ken correctly answered Iago, a character in the play *Othello*. It may have been the last time he answered a question on *Jeopardy!* Soon after the tournament, he said he didn't think he would compete on the show ever again.

Ken continues to write books and is active on Twitter. In 2017, he started a podcast with musician John Roderick. They tell strange, quirky stories from history. In 2020, he published a board game called Half Truth. Ken created the game with Richard Garfield, a mathematician and creator of Magic: The Gathering.

People often said Ken should host *Jeopardy!* someday. He usually responded that he didn't want to imagine the show without Alex Trebek. But in September 2020, he took a new position with

the show as a consulting producer, an ambassador for the program to conventions and other events. And after Trebek's death in November, Ken was asked to host a group of new *Jeopardy!* episodes.

In 2013, Ken spoke about his experience playing *Jeopardy!* against the supercomputer Watson. Ken said it made him feel awful to see a computer beat him at the thing he did best. He also spoke about how sad it would be if everyone gave up on learning facts just because computers could find information so easily. Ken argued that it's important for people to learn new things every day. Our shared knowledge connects us to one another.

Imagine a *Jeopardy!* clue that states: "He believes trivia can bring the world together." The correct question would be "Who is Ken Jennings?"

Timeline of Ken Jennings's Life

1974 — Kenneth Wayne Jennings III is born on May 23 in Edmonds, Washington

1992 — Attends the University of Washington for freshman year of college

1995 — Returns to United States after two years in Spain to attend Brigham Young University (BYU)

2000 — Marries fiancée Mindy Boam

2002 — Son Dylan is born

2004 — First *Jeopardy!* episode featuring Ken is broadcast on TV on June 2 and last episode airs on November 30

2005 — Comes in second in the *Jeopardy! Ultimate Tournament of Champions*

2006 — Publishes first book, *Brainiac: Adventures in the Curious, Competitive, Compulsive World of Trivia Buffs*

— Daughter Caitlin is born

2011 — Defeated by the IBM supercomputer Watson in a *Jeopardy!* event

2014 — Comes in second in *Jeopardy! Battle of the Decades*

2019 — Captains the second-place team in the *Jeopardy! All Star Games*

2020 — Wins the *Jeopardy! Greatest of All Time* tournament

Timeline of the World

1964 — The original run of the game *Jeopardy!* begins on US television, hosted by Art Fleming

1974 — US president Richard Nixon resigns from office

1977 — *Star Wars: A New Hope* premieres on May 25

1980 — Mount St. Helens, a volcano in Washington State, erupts on May 18, killing fifty-seven people

1984 — "Weird Al" Yankovic releases his song "I Lost on *Jeopardy!*"

1990 — The Hubble Space Telescope is launched

1997 — IBM's Deep Blue computer defeats chess master Garry Kasparov in a match

2004 — Facebook is launched

2007 — *Harry Potter and the Deathly Hallows*, the last Harry Potter book, is published

2010 — Burj Khalifa, the world's tallest building, opens in Dubai

2016 — The musical *Hamilton* opens on Broadway

2017 — The Women's March on Washington takes place on January 21

2020 — The Black Lives Matter movement gains recognition protesting the murders of George Floyd, Breonna Taylor, and others

Bibliography

Edwards, Alan. "Secrets of a 'Jeopardy' Winner Revealed,"
  Deseret News, January 13, 2005. https://www.deseret.
  com/2005/1/13/19871631/secrets-of-a-jeopardy-winner-
  revealed.

Ivie, Devon. "Reminiscing with Ken Jennings About His Intense First
  Jeopardy! Episode," ***Vulture***, May 4, 2020.

Jennings, Ken. ***Brainiac: Adventures in the Curious,***
  Competitive, Compulsive World of Trivia Buffs. New York:
  Villard, 2006.

Jennings, Ken. "Watson, Jeopardy, and Me, the Obsolete Know-It-
  All." Speech, ***TEDxSeattleU***, Seattle, WA, February 2013.

Lincoln, Kevin. "America's Hardest-Working Know-It-All,"
  BuzzFeed, February 14, 2013. https://www.buzzfeed.com/
  ktlincoln/americas-hardest-working-know-it-all.

Ready, Lauren. "Ken Jennings: "Greatest 'Jeopardy' Champ Tells
  All," ***USA Today***, November 20, 2013. https://www.usatoday.
  com/story/life/people/2013/11/20/ken-jennings-where-is-he-
  now/3633945/.

Rees, Bridget. "Who Is Ken Jennings?" *LDSLiving*, January 1, 2007. https://www.ldsliving.com/Who-is-Ken-Jennings-/s/5796.

Thorbecke, Catherine, Cameron Harrison, and Alyssa Ponce. "'Jeopardy!' Legend Ken Jennings Says It's 'Inevitable' He Will Face-off Against James Holzhauer," *Good Morning America*, June 6, 2019. https://abcnews.go.com/GMA/Culture/jeopardy-legend-ken-jennings-inevitable-face-off-james/story?id=63509249.

Uitti, Jacob. "Ken Jennings Talks Buzzer Strategy, Marvel Movies, and Alex Trebek," *Interview*, February 10, 2020.

Winters, Charlene Renberg. "Final Jeopardy," *BYU Magazine*, Winter 2005. https://magazine.byu.edu/article/final-jeopardy/.

Website

www.jeopardy.com

YOUR HEADQUARTERS FOR HISTORY

Activities, Mad Libs, and sidesplitting jokes!
Discover the Who HQ books beyond the biographies

Based on the New York Times Best-Selling Series
Knock! Knock! Who Was There?
OVER 300 sidesplitting jokes
by Brian Elling

Based on the New York Times Best-Selling Series
Knock! Knock! Where Is There?
OVER 300 sidesplitting jokes
by Brian Elling

The Who Was? Activity Book
Puzzles, Mazes & Tons of Fun
Based on the New York Times Best-Selling Series

Who Is _____? The Story of My Life
A Journal for You, by You!

Who Was? MAD LIBS
World's Greatest Word Game

Who? What? Where?

Learn more at whohq.com!